Dalai Lama Life and Teachings

Kousik Sastri

ISBN 978-93-5559-211-8

Published in India 2022 by Pencil

A brand of
One Point Six Technologies Pvt. Ltd.
123, Building J2, Shram Seva Premises,
Wadala Truck Terminal, Wadala (E)
Mumbai 400037, Maharashtra, INDIA
E connect@thepencilapp.com
W www.thepencilapp.com

Author biography

Retired Professor, writer, poet, has several publications in the form of books, papers etc.

CONTENTS

Dalai Lama Best Quotes

14th Dalai Lama, religious name: Tenzin Gayatso, abbreviated from Jetsun Jamefel Nagavang Lobsang Yehe Tenzin Gayato; Lamo Thandup was born, the current Dalai Lama. The Dalai Lama is an important monk of the Gelug school, the newest school of Tibetan Buddhism, officially led by Ganden Tripash. From the time of the Fifth Dalai Lama until 1959, the central government of Tibet, Ganden Fodarang, invested in the Dalai Lama's position on a temporary basis. She has traveled the world and talked about Tibetans' welfare, environment, economy, women's rights, non-violence, interfaith dialogue, physics, astronomy, Buddhism and science, cognitive neuroscience, reproductive health and sexuality. Mahayana and Vajrayana Buddhist teachings. Some of the best quotes from the Dalai Lama are listed below. "An orderly mind leads to happiness, and a disciplined mind leads to sorrow." - The Dalai Lama "A good friend who identifies mistakes and imperfections and rebukes evil should be respected as revealing the secrets of any hidden treasure." - The Dalai Lama “One spoon cannot taste the food it carries. Similarly, a foolish man, even if he associates with age, cannot understand the wisdom of a wise man. The Dalai Lama "True empathy for others does not change even if they treat you badly or hurt you" - Dalai Lama “All misery is due to ignorance. People hurt others for the sake of their own happiness or contentment "- Dalai Lama "While you may not always be able to avoid difficult situations, choosing how to respond to a situation can change the extent to which you suffer." - The Dalai Lama "Eye for eye ... we are all blind." - The Dalai Lama "Anger is the ultimate destroyer of your own peace of mind" - Dalai Lama "As human beings living today, we must consider future generations: a clean environment is a human right like any other human being. Therefore, it is part of our responsibility to make sure that the world we live in is healthier than the world we have passed, and if not healthier then it is part of our responsibility towards others "- Dalai Lama "When you are breathing, nurture yourself. Take care of all marriages as soon as you breathe out "- Dalai Lama "Glad to change your goal, but never change your value." - The Dalai Lama "Be kind whenever possible. It is always possible - the Dalai Lama "Because we will all divide this planet earth, we must learn to maintain unity and peace with each other and with nature. It is not just a dream, but a necessity." - Dalai Lama "It's better to be optimistic." - The Dalai Lama "Don't avoid liability for your actions." - The Dalai Lama "Never forget my silence for ignorance, my silence for acceptance or my exploitation for weakness. Compassion and tolerance are not signs of weakness, but of strength. - The Dalai Lama "Every day, as you wake up, think, today I am lucky to be alive, I have a precious human life, I will not waste it. I am going to use all my strength to develop myself, to extend my heart to others; Acquiring knowledge for the benefit of all people. I am going to think kindly of others, I will not be angry or think badly of others. I am going to benefit others as much as I can. The Dalai Lama "Follow three more: - Respect for yourself. - Respect for others. - Responsibility for all your actions." - Dalai Lama "Forget failure. Keep the text. "- The Dalai Lama "Those of you who love wings to fly, come back in the day and give reasons to stay." - The Dalai Lama "Given the scale of cosmic life, a human life is nothing more than a small blip. Each of us is a successful visitor to this planet, a guest who will only stay for a limited time. What could be more foolish than spending this short time alone, being dissatisfied or arguing with our peers? Enriched by the sense of our connection with others and the feeling of serving them, it is certainly better to use our short time here in meaningful living. "- The Dalai Lama "Happiness is more determined by the state of mind than by external events." - The Dalai Lama "It simply came to our notice then. It comes from your own actions. "- The Dalai Lama "Hard times build determination and inner strength. Through them we can also come to appreciate anger unnecessarily. Instead of being angry, instead of cultivating deep care and respect for the problem solvers, they give us invaluable opportunity to practice our tolerance and patience by creating such trying situations. The Dalai Lama "Human happiness and human satisfaction ultimately come from within" - Dalai Lama "Human potential is the same for everyone. Your feeling, "I have no value" is wrong. Absolutely wrong. You are fooling yourself. We all have the power to think - so what do you lack? If you have the will, you can change anything. It is commonly said that you are your own boss "- Dalai Lama "I believe that empathy is one of the few things we can practice that will bring immediate and long-term happiness to our lives. I have short-term pleasures like sex, drugs or gambling I'm not talking about contentment (although I'm shaking them), but something that will bring true and lasting happiness. That kind of stick. "- The Dalai Lama "When I make enemies my friends, I defeat them." - The Dalai Lama “I will not suggest to you that my path is the best. The decision is up to you. If you find some points that may be suitable for you, you can continue to experiment for yourself. If you see that it has no benefit, you can cancel it. - The Dalai Lama "If the problem is fixed, if there is a situation where you can do something about it, there is no need to worry. If it is not stable, there is no need to worry. There is no gain in thinking anyway. The Dalai Lama "If I am happy only for myself, the chances of happiness are very low. If I'm happy when good things happen to other people, there are billions more likely to be happy! "- The Dalai Lama "If it can be solved, there is no need to worry and if it cannot be solved, there is no need to worry" - Dalai Lama "If someone has a gun and tries to kill you, it would be reasonable to shoot with your own gun." - The Dalai Lama "Happiness will flow to us if we do nothing to stop our angry, intense and corrupt thoughts and emotions." - The Dalai Lama “If you can, help others; If you can't do that, at least don't hurt them. "" - Dalai Lama "If you don't love yourself, you can't love others. You cannot love another. If you have no compassion for yourself, you are not able to feel compassion for others. - The Dalai Lama "Even if you have primary concerns for others, failure can't bother you." - The Dalai Lama "If you have any concerns about pain or discomfort, you should check to see if there is anything you can do about it. No need to worry about it if you can; But if you can't do anything, don't worry. - The Dalai Lama "If you think you're too small to make a difference, try sleeping with a mosquito." - The Dalai Lama "If you think you're too small to make a difference, try sleeping with a mosquito." - The Dalai Lama "You want others to be happy, practice empathy. If you want to be happy, try to be empathetic." - The Dalai Lama "In general, if we observe a given situation very objectively and honestly, we realize that for the most part, we are also responsible for the unfolding of the event." - The Dalai Lama "To be rich, a person must first work very hard, so he must give up leisure time." - The Dalai Lama "We must create a positive vision here in order to take positive action." - The Dalai Lama "In our struggle for independence, the truth is our only weapon" - the Dalai Lama "The key to inner peace: if you have inner peace, external problems do not feel your depth and peace ... Without this inner peace your life is not as comfortable as it is materially, you may still be anxious, upset, or dissatisfied with the situation." - Dalai Lama "Instead of wondering why this is happening to you, consider why this is happening to you" Dalai Lama "It simply came to our notice then. If we make friends with ourselves, there is no barrier for us to open our hearts and minds to others "- Dalai Lama "We need to help others in our daily lives, not our prayers." - The Dalai Lama "It is in the greatest disadvantage that one is most likely to do good for oneself and others." - Dalai Lama "It's very rare or almost impossible that the phenomenon could be negative from all angles." - The Dalai Lama "Judge for yourself what you had to give up for your success" - Dalai Lama "Just a small positive thought in the morning can change your whole day." - The Dalai Lama "Know the rules well, so you can effectively break them." - The Dalai Lama "Let's try to identify the precious nature of each day." - The Dalai Lama "Look at the kids. Of course they can fight, but in general they do not feel sick until they grow up. Most adults have more education than children, but what good is an education if they have a big smile on their face, hiding their negative feelings? Children do not usually behave in this way. If they feel angry with someone, they express it and then it ends. The next day they can still play with that person. "- The Dalai Lama "Look at the situation from all angles and you will become more open." - The Dalai Lama "Love and compassion are necessities, not luxuries. Humanity cannot survive without them. "- Dalai Lama "My religion is very simple. My religion is kindness. - The Dalai Lama "No space station or enlightened mind can ever be realized." - The Dalai Lama "Old friend died, new friend appeared. It's just like the day. An old day is gone, a new day comes. The important thing is to make it meaningful: meaningful friend - or a meaningful day "- Dalai Lama Only the development of empathy and understanding towards others can bring us all peace and happiness all " - The Dalai Lama "Our ancient experience confirms at every stage that everything is connected, everything is inseparable" - Dalai Lama "Our lives are so dependent on others that we have a basic need for love at the root of our existence. That is why it is so important to have a clear idea of our responsibilities and our sincere concern for the well-being of others. "" - Dalai Lama "Our main purpose in life is to help others. And if you can't help them, at least don't hurt them. "" - The Dalai Lama "Pain can change you, but that doesn't mean it has to be a bad change. Take that pain and turn it into wisdom "- Dalai Lama "Peace does not mean the absence of conflict; There will always be differences. Peace means resolving these differences through peaceful means; Through dialogue, education, knowledge; And in a humane way. "- The Dalai Lama "People take different paths in search of fulfillment and happiness. Just because they're not on your street doesn't mean they're lost. "- The Dalai Lama "Remember that sometimes getting what you want is a great stroke of luck" - Dalai Lama "Remember that the best relationship is that your love for each other outweighs your need for each other" - Dalai Lama "Share your knowledge. It's a way to achieve immortality" - Dalai Lama "Silence is sometimes the best answer." - The Dalai Lama "If you want a smile from another face, smile" - Dalai Lama "You should not judge by someone else's actions." - Dalai Lama "Spend some time alone every day." - The Dalai Lama "Remember that great love and great accomplishments involve great risk." - The Dalai Lama "The best way to solve any problem in the human world is for all parties to sit down and talk" - Dalai Lama "The animals that live on this earth are humans or animals - they are here to contribute in their own way to the beauty and prosperity of the world." - The Dalai Lama The first step towards a happy life is to be kind to each other. "- Dalai Lama "The goal is not to be better than the other person, but your former self." - The Dalai Lama "The important thing is that men should have a purpose in life. It has to be something useful, something good. "- The Dalai Lama "The mind is like a parachute. It works best when it is exposed. "- The Dalai Lama "The more we care about the happiness of others, the more we feel good about ourselves ..." - Dalai Lama "The more you are inspired by love, the more fearless and free your actions will be." - The Dalai Lama "The more you cherish the feeling of loving compassion, the happier and calmer you will be" "- Dalai Lama "The motivation for all religious practices is the same: love, sincerity, honesty. The lives of virtually all religious people are harmonious. The teachings of tolerance, love and affection are the same. "- The Dalai Lama "The purpose of all major religious traditions is not to build large temples on the outside, but to build temples of kindness and compassion in the heart" - Dalai Lama "The ultimate source of happiness is that we focus on our inner values." - The Dalai Lama "The way to change the mind of others is not affection, not anger." - The Dalai Lama "There are always problems to be faced, but it makes a difference when we have a calm mind." - The Dalai Lama "There are only two days in a year that nothing can be done. One is called yesterday and the other is called tomorrow. Today is the perfect day to love, trust, tax and live most of the time. - The Dalai Lama "There is a saying in Tibetan, 'Tragedy should be used as a source of energy.' Whatever the difficulties, whatever the painful experience, if we lose our hope, this is our real disaster. "- The Dalai Lama "Just one important thing you should keep in mind and let it be your guide. What people tell you is who you are. Keep this true. You must ask yourself if you want to live your own life. We live and we die, it is true that we can only face each other. No one can help us, not even the Buddha. So consider carefully, what prevents you from living the way you want to live your life? "- The Dalai Lama "This is my simple religion. We don't need temples; we don't need complex philosophy. We have our own brains, our own hearts are our temples; philosophy is compassionate" - Dalai Lama "Time flies. When we make a mistake we can't turn the clock around and try again. All we can do is make the most of the present. - The Dalai Lama "Winning the war is a bigger victory than winning a thousand" - Dalai Lama "A much more self-centered attitude, you see, bring, see, isolation. Consequences: loneliness, fear, anger. Extreme self-centeredness is the source of suffering. - The Dalai Lama "It simply came to our notice then. Leave it as it is outside. - The Dalai Lama "But we are the visitors of this planet. We've been here for a hundred years or so. During this time, we must try to do something good that is relevant to our lives. If you agree with other people's happiness, you will find the real goal, the real meaning of life. - The Dalai Lama "We can never have peace in the outside world unless we have peace with ourselves." - The Dalai Lama "It simply came to our notice then We don't need money, we don't need more success or fame, we don't need perfect body or even perfect partner. Right now, at the moment, we have the mind, which is all the basic tools we need to achieve complete happiness. "" - Dalai Lama "We need to make a concerted effort to build the positive aspects in us." - The Dalai Lama "We need to learn how we want what we want in order to have lasting and stable happiness." - The Dalai Lama "We have to learn what we have to have stable and unwavering happiness, we have not got what we want." - The Dalai Lama "What is the meaning of life? To be happy and useful." - Dalai Lama "I am most surprised by the" man "because he sacrifices his health to make money. He then gave up money for his own health. And then he is so anxious about the future that he does not enjoy the present; The result is that he does not live in the present or in the future; He lives as if he never dies, and then never really dies' - Dalai Lama "When life gets too complicated and we feel overwhelmed, it is often helpful to stand back and remind ourselves of our overall goal, our overall goal. Faced with feelings of stagnation and confusion, this will bring us what true happiness is and it may be helpful to take just an hour, an afternoon or even a few days to reset our priorities based on that. It can bring our lives back to the right context, approve a new perspective and enable us to see which direction to take. "- The Dalai Lama "When we fall into a destructive emotion, we have our greatest asset: our freedom." - The Dalai Lama "When we can no longer change the situation, we are challenged to change ourselves." - The Dalai Lama "When we feel love and compassion for others, it not only makes us feel loved and cared for, but it also helps us to develop inner happiness and peace." - The Dalai Lama "When we are confronted with the real tragedy of life, we can respond in two ways - either by losing hope and falling into the habit of self-destruction or by using the challenge of finding our inner strength." - The Dalai Lama "If you lose, don't lose the lesson." - The Dalai Lama "When you realize you have made a mistake, take immediate action to correct it" - Dalai Lama "When you speak, you are simply repeating what you already know; But when you listen, you can learn something new. - The Dalai Lama "When you think that everything is someone else's fault, you will suffer a lot. When you realize that everything starts with yourself, you will learn both peace and joy. - The Dalai Lama "With a sense of accomplishment and confidence in one's own abilities, one can build a better world." - The Dalai Lama "It is impossible to be blessed without your efforts." - The Dalai Lama "World peace must develop from internal peace. Peace is not just the absence of violence. Peace, I think, is a manifestation of human affection. ”- The Dalai Lama

Dalai Lama and His Teachings

How can I stay calm, if I am always wrong? To establish one's own peace with oneself, one needs to be able to see the mistakes correctly. The Dalai Lama said he would take action to correct the mistake. Unnecessary worries are of no consequence if no problem is solved.

Time flows smoothly. When we make a mistake, we can't stop trying. All we can do is make good use of the present tense.

It is important to remember that great love and great achievement involve great risk. Risk and danger, part of life.

Assessing each day, the risks and dangers become fluid. The Dalai Lama said, "Let's try to realize the importance of each day."

4) The relationship between 'happiness and word of mouth'

The relationship between happiness and conversation is intense. We can build relationships by talking, and by talking we can break the long-standing relationship forever. I can inspire by talking, I can stop someone permanently by talking.

Many times we are not relieved until we have given the right word / proper answer. I am satisfied after saying that. But that satisfaction is very temporary. The discomfort will start a little after saying the right thing - guilt will be created. I think it was better not to say. Just as saliva cannot be taken back, so spoken cannot be brought back.

The keynote at a talk show came in the form of a question: What builds or destroys your speech?

Just as it is important to speak at the appropriate time, it is also important to remain silent or not to speak at the appropriate time. Rabindranath said, 'Go and talk a lot, don't say a word.'

The Dalai Lama says people are fascinated by talking too much; Significant fascination can be created even from the silent. Silence is often considered the best answer.

We can build others by talking. A positive attitude is needed here. Being able to perceive the positive side of others is a valuable quality. The Dalai Lama said that the seeds of all good are produced in the land of praise.

5) Happiness and non-discrimination: All people are equal, everyone's needs are the same

The Dalai Lama has given excellent arguments for creating solidarity among people of all races. It is almost impossible to refute it. Whatever can be refuted, it cannot be avoided.

There are as many causes of violence as there are differences between people. People are one in all aspects of natural, geographical, scientific. What is the proof that man is one? All of them have the same physical and emotional needs. Their goals and expectations are the same.

The Dalai Lama says: rich or poor, educated or illiterate, pious or unbeliever, male or female, white or black, we are all one. We are all equal physically, emotionally and mentally. We all have basic needs like food, shelter, security and emotions. We all want to avoid happiness and misery. We all have hopes, worries, fears and dreams. Everyone wants their family and loved ones to be well. When we lose something we are sad and when we gain something we are happy. In this place, religion, ethnic identity, culture and language make no difference between us.

Because of social inequalities, our behavior is not the same for everyone. We are also reluctant to call you an old rickshaw puller, but the young man in sophisticated clothes is addressed as 'you'. Let us preserve the sweetness of our good behavior and words for special people on special days. Therefore, there is a reason for happiness in being able to see all people equally!

7) Happiness and religion: The relationship of morality with religion

According to the Dalai Lama, religion or institution cannot separate people. People are one here too. Everyone wants happiness. So everyone has to practice empathy and kindness. Mercy is religion.

"My religion is very simple," he said. There is no need for a house of worship for this. No complex philosophy required. Dharmagraha is your mind and your heart. Your philosophy is kindness.

According to him, the main purpose of religious traditions is not to establish a shrine on the side of the road, but to establish goodness and compassion in our hearts.

The overall purpose of religion is to promote love and compassion, patience, tolerance, humility and forgiveness.

To establish

"People live without religion and meditation, but we cannot survive without human qualities," he said.

Therefore, kindness or compassion is not a religious issue, it is a human trait. It is not a luxury, but a necessity for our own peace and emotional well-being. It is necessary for human existence. This is about the Dalai Lama.

How reasonable is it to despise people or think differently with religion? The Dalai Lama says people walk different paths for happiness and success. Just because someone is walking your path does not mean that they are destroyed.

According to him, religion can be different. Or religion may not exist. But morality is not just a religious quality. The Dalai Lama said, "In today's society, I think there is a need to find a universal and sustainable way to achieve morality, inherent values and personal integrity." Because these qualities transcend religious, cultural, and ethnographic differences. I call it secular morality.

"I don't think morality requires religion or religious beliefs," he said. Rather I firmly believe that the issue of morality comes naturally and rationally considering humanities and human conditions.

8) Happiness and education: The expectation that should be from education

The problem with our current society is their expectations about education. They think that learning will make them smarter and more intelligent. Even though our society does not view education that way, the most important purpose of education and knowledge is to involve oneself in better deeds and to establish discipline within the mind.

The proper application of our knowledge and growth is to change within ourselves to establish a good heart.

I think ignorance is the cause of human suffering. People hurt others in search of their own happiness and satisfaction as selfish. But real happiness comes from inner happiness and contentment. This happiness comes from kindness, love and kindness. It comes as a result of abandoning ignorance, selfishness and greed.

What is ignorance? Lack of proper guidance on the source of happiness. What is the source of happiness? Kindness, love and kindness. How is kindness, love and kindness possible? Through knowledge acquisition, selfless mind and unselfish heart.

What is the result of education? The ability to involve oneself in good deeds and to establish a good heart.

The spoon can never taste the food he carries. Even if he gets the company of a saint in the same way, the fool cannot understand it. Says the Dalai Lama.

Dalai Lama: Relevant identity

All discussions are about the fourteenth Dalai Lama Tenzin Geatsuke (1935-). Tenzin Geatsu has gained more popularity and universality than any of his predecessors. People line up to buy tickets to learn from his life and philosophy. Combining the philosophies of the Mahatma, Mandela and, above all, the Buddha, he has come up with a universal explanation for which he is a popular speaker around the world. His philosophy is now the subject of university lessons.

The first reason for this is that he has been able to bring people to a uniform level and to promote the universality of morality. The essence of his philosophy is man and his common human needs. As a result, people have been able to discover themselves in the teachings of the Dalai Lama.

Another reason is that by recognizing different religions and being able to highlight its main purpose, it is: the pursuit of human happiness.

In the present text, the Dalai Lama is seen as a secular philosopher, not as a religious or political leader. His philosophy of happiness is based on a strong argument that there is a mixture of spiritual and worldly consciousness. Despite his religious identity, he has placed his thinking in a neutral position, where religious differences are irrelevant. The hegemony of the Dalai Lama has united all believers and unbelievers as human beings.

The fourteenth Dalai Lama is the exception. Although the Dalai Lama has been their spiritual and political leader in Tibet's centuries-old religious tradition, the 14th Dalai Lama paved the way for the formation of a democratic government in Tibet (2011). Although he considers himself only a spiritual guru, he is fighting for the freedom of the people of Tibet in a non-violent way. He recently announced that he no longer needed the Dalai Lama.

Religion and Terrorism

The Dalai Lama, the spiritual leader of Tibet, said, "There is no such thing as a Muslim or a Christian terrorist. When a person becomes a terrorist, regardless of his religion, he leaves the religion. " The Dalai Lama is the spiritual leader of Tibet. The Dalai Lama, the spiritual leader of Tibet, said, "When someone catches terror, he has no religion." He made the remarks at a public reception for the Dalai Lama in Imphal, the capital of the Indian state of Manipur, on Wednesday. "There is no such thing as a Muslim or a Christian terrorist," he said. When a person becomes a terrorist, regardless of his religion, he leaves the religion from that moment on. The Dalai Lama said the religious beliefs of different people and communities differ. However, no one has the right to convert or preach to people of other religions. At the time, he called the violence against the Muslim Rohingya in Myanmar "unfortunate" and condemned religious intolerance around the world. The 62-year-old exiled Tibetan spiritual leader has been in India since 1959.

Every care has been taken to make the book accurate, however if there is any error, it is only incidental and unwanted or typing errors.

Some Issues

The Dalai Lama, Tibet's spiritual leader, says all religions carry messages of love. But the problem is politicians. Now politics is also being done with religion. The Dalai Lama spoke on various issues at the press conference. Issues such as the persecution of minorities in China and the Taiwan crisis have come up for discussion. At the time, the question was whether the international community would consider boycotting the Winter Olympics in China due to the persecution of minorities. In response, the Dalai Lama said, "I have known Communist Party leaders since the time of Mao Zedong. Their thinking is good. At times, however, they become more extreme, strictly controlling. 'The spiritual leader added,' When it comes to Tibet and Xinjiang, we have our own culture. The narrow-minded Chinese communist leaders do not understand this diversity of different cultures. ' The Dalai Lama has accused the Han, China's largest community, of exerting excessive control over other groups. He says it's not just the Han people who are in China. Many other communities also live here. The Dalai Lama also spoke at a press conference on the Taiwan issue. China considers Taiwan as part of its mainland. But Taiwan has been claiming itself as an independent sovereign state. The crisis is going on. The Dalai Lama believes that Taiwan is a treasure trove of ancient Chinese culture and heritage. But now politics is being done with this region. At the end of the press conference, the leader said that all religions bring a message of love. Different perspectives on philosophy have been presented in all religions. Now the problem is the politicians, in some cases the economists too. They are using this difference of religion. Religion is also being politicized. That's a problem. Meanwhile, the Dalai Lama is currently in India. He described the country as a center of religious harmony. According to the Dalai Lama, he wants to live in "peace" in India. In his address to the EU Parliament, the Dalai Lama emphasized the importance of friendly relations and mutual trust with China. He also ruled out the possibility of separating Tibet from China Clearly, I want to make it clear that our movement is not for isolation We want real autonomy It is good for us to be with a big country like China We want to maintain social harmony, stability and unity It is much easier to achieve goals through mutual respect and loyalty, not guns Expressing solidarity with the Tibetans, he welcomed the decision by some EU parliamentarians to go on hunger strike. The Dalai Lama's 20-minute speech in the EU Parliament was as serious as his personal experience. The 63-year-old spiritual leader did not even forget to joke That is why the President of the EU Parliament, Hans-Geert Poetering, has called the Dalai Lama a champion of dialogue. At the same time, he said it was now the EU's responsibility to put pressure on China to establish democracy, human rights, freedom of speech and fundamental rights. The Dalai Lama is visiting Europe at a time when tensions between China and the EU are running high. China canceled a meeting with the EU last week The conference was scheduled to take place in Leo,

France on Monday The Dalai Lama is scheduled to hold talks with French President Nicolas Sarkozy in Poland during his European tour. China has also warned France about this On Thursday, the Chinese Foreign Ministry made it clear that China has strategic and trade relations with France. Two things are very important So only if bilateral relations are good will China create a conducive trade environment

A Great Life

The Dalai Lama is the spiritual head of Tibet. He is the top official in the Tibetan constitution. According to Tibetan beliefs, the Dalai Lama is the incarnation of the compassionate Bodhisattva Avalokiteshvara. He is a person of royal status in Tibet. The current fourteenth Dalai Lama is Tenzin Giatsu. The Dalai Lama is the title of the religious leader of Tibet, the once forbidden kingdom on the roof of the world. In Tibet, the branch of Buddhism called 'Gelug', the main religious leader is called Dalai Lama. In Mongolian the word 'Dalai' means sea and in Sanskrit 'lama' means guru or spiritual teacher. That is, the full meaning of the word Dalai Lama is a teacher whose knowledge or spirituality is as deep as the sea. On the other hand, the word Giatsu is associated with the Dalai Lama's name. For example, the name of the current Dalai Lama is Tenzin Giatsu. The word 'giatsu' in Tibetan also means sea. That word is actually synonymous with the Dalai Lama. The present Dalai Lama was born into a peasant family in the village of Taksar in the northeastern province of Amdo, Tibet. Born on July 7, 1935, the 14th Dalai Lama has 15 more siblings. The two-year-old was initially selected as the Dalai Lama when the country's senior religious leaders found signs of him becoming a Dalai Lama and the country's administrator. He was then placed in a Buddhist monastery under the supervision of veteran religious leaders. He later earned a doctorate in Buddhist philosophy. Today, the Dalai Lama is the name of a person whose name is being uttered all over the world. Due to his charismatic personality, calm majestic figure, ever smiling face, message of peace and non-violence on his face, etc., he is now not only a religious leader of Tibetans, but a person who has earned the respect of people all over the world. Dalai Lama's educational life Education began at the age of seven in the capital, Lhasa, under the chief lamas. In 1959 he completed the highest education in Buddhist philosophy. Young Dalai Lama; Already in 1950, China occupied Tibet. But in March 1959, the people of Tibet took to the streets to regain their autonomy and clashed with the Chinese army. Thousands of Tibetans were killed. The Dalai Lama was ousted from his residence, Potala Palace. When the Dalai Lama migrated to India from Tibet, the Indian government gave him asylum. The Tibetan leader has always spoken of compromise and non-violence to avoid conflict with China. The leader has been urging thousands of angry Tibetan lamas and millions of followers to calmly protest against the Chinese government's injustice. The Dalai Lama is preaching non-violence around the world; Despite being exiled from his homeland, in the last days of his life, this leader is conveying the message of non-violence to the world. For this he was awarded the Nobel Peace Prize in 1989. Let the words of non-violence of the Dalai Lama remain as unwavering in the faith and belief of ordinary Tibetans living in the lap of the Himalayas as the Himalayas do. He has visited more than 50 countries of the world one or more times so far. The one who started his foreign tour in 1967 still exists today. He often meets or sometimes joins in stories with statesmen from around the world, including Canada, the United States and Europe. Besides, he participated in important discussions in various seminars at the invitation of world renowned universities. He is also seen giving important speeches in seminars of Jadrel scientists and researchers from different countries. He has also been awarded honorary doctorates from several universities. The Dalai Lama is the spiritual head of Tibet. He is the top official in the Tibetan constitution. According to Tibetan beliefs, the Dalai Lama is the incarnation of the compassionate Bodhisattva Avalokiteshvara. He is a person of royal status in Tibet. The Dalai Lama lives in the luxurious Potala Palace in Lhasa, Tibet. The current 14th Dalai Lama is Tenzin Giatsu. After the annexation of Tibet by China, the 14th Dalai Lama, along with some of his followers, secretly left the country and came to India in 1958 and took refuge there. He has won the Nobel Peace Prize for his contributions to peace in Tibet. The present Dalai Lama was born into a peasant family in the village of Taksar in the northeastern province of Amdo, Tibet. Born on July 7, 1935, The two-year-old was initially elected Dalai Lama after senior religious leaders in the country found signs that he was the Dalai Lama and the country's administrator. The Dalai Lama's family name is Tenzin Giatsu. He was then placed in a Buddhist monastery under the supervision of veteran religious leaders. He later earned a doctorate in Buddhist philosophy. The Dalai Lama is today the name of a person whose name is being uttered in all circles of the world. Due to his charismatic personality, calm majestic figure, ever smiling face, message of peace and non-violence on his face, etc., he has now become a person who not only greets Tibetans but also people all over the world. He has visited more than 50 countries of the world one or more times so far. The one who started his foreign tour in 1967 still exists today. He often meets or sometimes joins in stories with statesmen from around the world, including Canada, the United States and Europe. In addition to the world's b Yatnama participated in important discussions at various seminars at the invitation of universities. He is also seen giving important speeches in seminars of Jadrel scientists and researchers from different countries. He has also been awarded honorary doctorates from several universities. The Dalai Lama is the title of the religious leader of Tibet, the once forbidden kingdom on the roof of the world. In Tibet, the branch of Buddhism called 'Gelug', the main religious leader is called Dalai Lama. In Mongolian the word 'Dalai' means sea and in Sanskrit 'lama' means guru or spiritual teacher. That is, the full meaning of the word Dalai Lama is a teacher whose knowledge or spirituality is as deep as the sea. On the other hand, the word Giatsu is associated with the Dalai Lama's name. For example, the name of the current Dalai Lama is Tenzin Giatsu. The word 'giatsu' in Tibetan also means sea. That word is actually synonymous with the Dalai Lama. But then how did the word Dalai Lama originate? Let's find out who is this Dalai Lama? The Dalai Lama is associated with the history of the rise of Buddhism in Tibet. From the 7th to the 9th century, the descendants of Sanjen began to increase in size with the neighboring Chinese Empire. The state of Tibet was established in the middle of the ninth century as one of the most powerful kingdoms in Central Asia. Conflicts with neighboring China continue to escalate. So in 622 AD,

Tibet signed a peace treaty with China to avoid a border conflict. The state of Tibet on the world map; Buddhism first began to spread in Tibet in the fifth century. But Buddhism did not spread much in Tibet before the eighth century. In the eighth century, King Trisang Dasten became interested in Buddhism and gave it the status of a monarchy. At the king's invitation, Buddhist monks from China and India flocked to the royal court in Tibet. At the same time, under the patronage of the king, the spread of Buddhism in Tibet began. But at that time, the people of Tibet believed in a religion called 'Bon'. 'Forest' is a symbol of religion; According to some historians, the followers of the 'forest' religion and the priests were outraged by this incident. Revolts broke out in various parts of Tibet over their clashes with Buddhists. Civil war broke out across Tibet as it failed to quell simultaneous uprisings in various parts of the vast kingdom. The rebels established small independent empires in various parts of war-torn Tibet. However, in the areas adjacent to China and India in Tibet, the number of Buddhists continues to increase. According to Lama and Dalai Lama Buddhist historians in Tibet, there was a follower of the Buddha named Avalokitesavra, who promised the Buddha that he would bring the light of the Buddha's teachings to the people of the foothills of the Himalayas. His followers later came to Lhasa in Tibet from India at the invitation of the King of Tibet and established a Buddhist learning center. Its teachers were known as 'lamas'. The eldest of the lamas was entrusted with all the responsibilities of the educational center. The civil war in Tibet led to the collapse of the whole of Tibet, and the widespread propagation of Buddhism throughout Tibet gradually reduced the power of Tibet to the hands of the chief lamas. Scene of the blessing of the Tibetan lamas; Read More: India's Best Cancer Hospital || Best Cancer Hospital in India 2021 | The best cancer specialist in India In 1261, the Mongol emperor Kublai Khan established the Yuan Empire in China. Tibet also came under the control of the gradually growing Yuan Empire. In 1579, the then Yuan Emperor Atlan Khan invited Sonam Giatsu, the then head of the Buddhist lama in Tibet, to meet him. However, the chief lama sent some of his disciples to the royal court of Altan Khan instead. His disciples returned to him and told him about the interest of Altan Khan and his kingdom members in Buddhism. Finally, in 156, Sonam Giatsu came to the court of Atlan Khan. Atalan Khan was fascinated by the knowledge and wisdom of Sonam Giatsu and gave her the title of Dalai Lama. Dalai Lama with Emperor Atlan Khan; According to Tibetan Buddhists, the chief lama, Gendun Drup, was born for the third time through Sonam Giatsu. So Sonam Giatsu is originally referred to as the Third Dalai Lama. In addition to the title of Dalai Lama, Atlan Khan also handed over the governing power of Tibet to them. In 1842, during the reign of the fifth Dalai Lama, Lobsang Giatsur, some reforms were introduced in the power of the Dalai Lama. For 365 years since then, the Dalai Lama has been the sole spiritual and religious guru of Tibet, leaving the power of Tibet unchanged. Is the Dalai Lama elected? Not through an election, but after the death of one Dalai Lama, following another miracle, another Dalai Lama was found. So far 14 Dalai Lamas have been found in the history of Tibet. According to the Buddhist 'Gelug' branch of Tibet, the Dalai Lama once died but was reborn again and again. This rebirth is to enlighten the future people of the world in the light of Buddha's teachings. So with the death of a Dalai Lama, the chief lamas of Tibet came together and began searching for the new Dalai Lama-like child. The Dalai Lama was originally found in three processes. The dream of the chief lamas: After the death of a Dalai Lama, one of the chief lamas gets an indication of what to do to find the baby Dalai Lama in their dream. The child Dalai Lama was found out by working accordingly. Following the path of smoke: If one of the chief lamas does not receive any instructions in a dream, the lamas follow the course of the smoke emitted during the funeral of the previous Dalai Lama. Following in the footsteps of that wash, they went from house to house trying to find the Dalai Lama in the newborn baby. Meditation on the shores of a lake called Lamo-la-so: When no other process can find the baby Dalai Lama, the lamas begin to meditate on the shores of a mountainous lake called Lamo-la-so. There are many myths in Tibet about this 2 sq km lake located at an altitude of 5,300 meters. Of the mysterious 'Lamo-la-so' lake; However, according to Tibetan Buddhists, the lake goddess Palden Lamo first promised the Dalai Lama that she would continue the Dalai Lama's rebirth. So the chief lamas continued to meditate until they received any indication of the infant Dalai Lama. After the death of the present 13th Dalai Lama in 1935, the chief lamara meditated for four years to find his successor, Tenzin Giatsu. At the age of 4, the Lamas found out about him and found him. After the child finds the Dalai Lama, he is presented with some of the items used by the previous Dalai Lama, among other things. If that child chooses something used by the previous Dalai Lama, then he will be considered as the next Dalai Lama. However, the Dalai Lama's search is limited to Tibet.